TOO BUSY, TOO BORED FOR PRAYER

GREEN RESOURCES

CONCETTA M. GREEN

TOO BUSY, TOO BORED FOR PRAYER

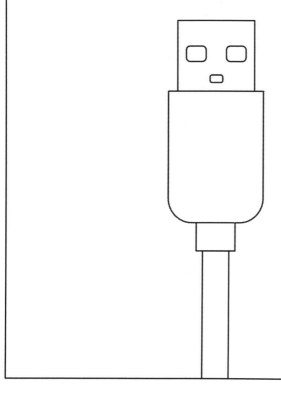

Cover Design: Jaron Green and Concetta Green
Interior Design: Phillip Gessert
Author Photo: Rene Tirado of Tirado Photography

NOTE: Some of the names in this book, as well as some identifying details have been changed to protect the anonymity of the people involved.

ISBN-10:0-9989749-0-0
ISBN-13:978-0-9989749-0-3

First Edition
Printed in the United States of America

ACKNOWLEDGMENTS

Thank you…
God, for letting me ask annoying questions and answering them all.
Jaron Green, for being my biggest supporter.
Dr. Charrise Barron, for being my friend and making sure the world saw this.
Tonya Bluston, Trisha Alcisto, and Sarah Fox, for editing.
My Prayer Circle, Tracy Harwood, Pam Lagomarsino of Above the Pages,
and Nicki Bishop, for being my very first readers.
Alina Lopez & Dorothy Grooms, for everything.
Jody Yeskey and Marta Melo, for opening my artistic eye.
Nicole Bolin, for being yourself.

TABLE OF CONTENTS

INTRODUCTION

INSTEAD of writing a book for people to read about prayer, I wanted to create a guide to help them *experience* it. I get distracted easily sometimes. Perhaps you do too. This book exists to help people like us revive our connection with God by learning how to focus our attention in prayer. With the right tools and some creativity, you will find or rediscover the joys of time invested in God. Without focused prayer, we miss out on a deeply personal connection to the eternal in our everyday life. Trust me, once you have had a taste of that connection, you won't want to give it up!

I also wrote this guide because sometimes I feel too busy to pray. Even though I speak publicly and have served as a pastor, there are times when it's difficult to make myself sit down and focus on anything. Especially prayer. When I wrote the first part of this book, I was coleading a church, working a full-time job, and managing a family. I was so preoccupied with life's endless to-do list that prayer became predictable and boring. I had plenty of needs to take to the Lord in prayer, but it seemed like so much work to actually get there! I found myself putting it off as long as possible because it felt like another chore. Fed up, I asked the Lord for ways to change my prayer life. I wanted it to come alive and mean something again. I wanted it to be fun; something I could look forward to. When I opened my heart and began to research the topic, the Lord gave me some cool ideas worth sharing. What made them worth sharing was that when I used them personally, they worked.

I could keep my thoughts focused long enough to pray in a meaningful way.

Humans look for patterns that allow us to function on autopilot most days. While rote systems are efficient at first, especially in business, on a personal level, they can quickly turn into a mindless routine. Specifically, as it relates to prayer, you may have taken this approach without even realizing it. Think about it: When was the last time you changed your form of daily prayer? During times of worship and prayer, do you find your mind wandering while your mouth repeats lyrics or familiar phrases over and over? Do you find yourself thinking about prayer and reasons why you should do it later? Do you get to your prayer time and realize you don't know what to say? Do you ever plan time for prayer anymore?

Your prayer life should make you better. It shouldn't become a time-card experience where you show up and put your time in, all the while thinking about how soon you get to leave. You shouldn't be bored. When you are in the space of prayer, it should be a workshop where the Lord speaks and you listen. You should be able to bring your concerns and those of others to lay at His feet. You should come away changed by small moments of insight with the Holy Spirit. And it doesn't have to take hours and hours. I want you to be happy once again, or maybe for the first time, with your prayer experience. I want you to read this book and deepen your relationship with the Lord.

In my search for a better prayer life, I learned to set up creative parameters with built-in accountability to get or keep myself spiritually healthy. Pushing myself and a friend to pray differently for seven days was eye-opening. In order to reset our spiritual lives, we had to accept the challenge of addressing our disconnection with God. I began to call the process the prayer challenge. The prayer challenge outlined in this book is meant to wipe out boredom and jump-start your prayer life. It is meant to give you a sample of different prayer styles and study tools so you can find what works best for you. Try it when you hit a wall or have a need spiritually and you will notice positive changes in your prayer time. The goal is to get you *praying* and to *enjoy it*!

Before we jump in, this challenge assumes a few things:

1. You have a personal relationship with Jesus Christ as your Lord and Savior.
2. You are connected to other believers through a church or Bible study.
3. You have access to the internet for websites, apps, and other digital resources.

I can confess that almost every book I've read about prayer has put me to sleep. Sorry, not sorry. I would get excited about the first few chapters, post about the book online or tell a friend, open the book, and promptly succumb to some zzz's. Weeks later, when I would accidentally knock over the book while reaching for something else, I would feel like a loser and binge-watch some television.

The problem I found with many books about prayer was that they were too abstract for my needs. I knew that I needed to pray. I *wanted* to pray. I was constantly searching for something that would *let* me pray right away.

Have you ever heard of the jump rope style called double Dutch? Double Dutch is a complicated form of jump rope that uses two ropes swinging in alternate directions simultaneously. To get in the middle, you must find the rhythm of the ropes and slide in between them without losing a beat or you will get hit. If you have never played double Dutch, the concept of jumping inside the two ropes can seem impossible.

In the same way, a lot of the books I read about prayer wouldn't let me jump right in. The structure always left me feeling confused and defeated. I never knew quite where to start, and the language seemed so philosophical and impractical that my eyes would glaze over sections. I needed something personal that would make me dig within myself. That said, I want you to use this book to *actually pray*—not just have an intellectual discussion about it. My goal is to keep this resource light and user-friendly for you.

YOU WILL NEED A PARTNER

The first time I shared these steps was during a lesson I taught on prayer at church. I wanted to offer something practical that people could actually *do* to change their prayer lives. I didn't want just another lecture on why one's prayer life matters. As part of the challenge, I asked participants to team up in groups of two. Their job was to pray separately and together for seven days following the guide I created.

For one week, I asked everyone to carefully consider the amount of time spent online and their choice of words used in daily interactions. This created a level of mindfulness of where time and mental energy were being spent. Then I asked them to connect with their partner for the seven days in person, via telephone, or video call. No texting was allowed for their daily check-ins. Crazy, right? Stay with me here!

Texting is my favorite because it's so easy and fast. But hearing the emotion in the voice of someone you're sitting down with or having a phone conversation with allows you to focus on the moment. There is giving and taking in healthy conversation and exchange of listening, hearing, sharing. Rediscovering that rhythm in your communication—taking turns to listen, breathe, and then speak—is excellent practice for your personal prayer life.

For this challenge to work, you have to break from the norm and go a little deeper with your partner. Developing in your Christian walk is always more fun when you have someone to walk with. The challenge partners served as built-in cheerleaders for one another. I also wanted to be sure that our members were learning how to pray audibly with another person, considering someone else's concerns along with their own, as they spoke to God.

At the end of seven days, we all returned to church and the testimonies were astounding. Several teams volunteered to come to the front and share their experiences. We heard from people who were glad for the chance to connect personally with other church members they did not previously know. Others shared how they felt spiritually awakened and revived by the challenge. It seemed that using their own creativity with a very basic plan made them feel joy that many had never experienced. The Scriptures held new weight in relation to everyday life and needs. They *got* it.

After service, I learned that people who struggled the most were those who chose to go it alone or who decided not to ask questions when they felt stuck. It was clear that each person needed a partner for this challenge. Think of it as having a spiritual workout buddy with whom you can check in daily for a week. Having a challenge partner creates built-in support during good times and bad times.

GROWING THE HABIT OF PRAYER

Thoughts, as you know, can be either healthy or unhealthy. Change first begins as a seed of thought. When that seed becomes an action, growth takes place. The question today is: are you choosing to nurture the seeds of life or of death (Jas. 1 NLT)?

In the modern world, we spend much of our time overstimulated by electronics and media. Most of us lie down in the dark, staring at bright screens and hoping that sleep or a cramp will override our need to watch "just one more episode." This kind of behavior reinforces the belief that change can come only from *yet another* external stimulus. Change begins from within. An active choice that distances you from a genuine connection with God is a step. And it ain't toward life. Each polite "No, thank you" given to the Holy Spirit is bringing you down. It's so tricky, though! Why? Because you don't realize how far away you truly are until a crisis hits, and you're totally at a loss as to how the Lord wants you to respond.

But today's distance doesn't mean you can't get your focus back. You can start saying "Yes, Lord" to the tugs on your heart to spend time with Him in prayer.

I don't know about you, but I can't always condense my issues and worries to the hour that a therapist charges. And with all the planning it takes to have an actual phone call these days, I can't wear out my friends with all my needs. Who has patience for that?

Well, God does. And He doesn't just listen, He speaks back. Good stuff, too!

Through some pretty dark valleys in my life, prayer has brought God's light: His hope, His clarity, and His peace. Dedicated time in active prayer has also opened up my creativity like never before. Walking this road for one solid week, you should expect greater clarity of mind with a few *aha* moments along the way. Each day's challenge is crafted to develop a different element of personal discipline, giving your prayer time shape and purpose.

Let's get to it.

HOW TO USE
THIS GUIDE

C ONSIDER this book as a seven-day spiritual fitness trainer. When you start the habit of working out at the gym, you've got to consistently learn new methods to keep yourself interested and challenged, right? In the same way, when you begin the habit of prayer, it will need intentional variety to keep it interesting. This challenge will help you to bring vibrancy to your prayer life.

Each day you will have:

- One task to complete alone
- One phone conversation with your partner
- One short reading for reflection and to guide your daily discussion

What you will need:

- A desire to connect with God personally
- An open heart and mind
- Access to a Bible
- Internet access
- A journal and pen

Other suggested items:

- Plain or colorful index cards

- Highlighters, markers, or colored pencils
- A container to hold your supplies (a basket, bag, or box)
  This lets you make a prayer space anywhere in minutes

TIPS FOR YOUR TEAM:

The day before your challenge officially begins, read page 9:
Prayer: How & When?

Determine in your mind that building a better connection with God
is possible.

Select a partner who is as dedicated to the prayer challenge as you are.

Discuss the personal challenge and devotional of the day and how they
affected you. Then ask, "How can I pray for you today?" Write down
their answer and pray for one another before hanging up.

Sacrifice something during the seven days as a fast—a type of food or
drink, time online, spending, etc. Devote that time instead to
journaling observations made during the challenge or doing something
to feed your spiritual side (for ideas, see "Resources" on page 73).

Avoid consuming media that contains harsh content. Surround yourself
with Christian music or wholesome audio content that you *enjoy*! What
you feed your subconscious matters!

Protect your challenge partner by not sharing his or her private
concerns with others. Your prayers should be rooted in love, always
willing to protect the vulnerable, never boasting, not envious, and not
finding fault. Remember that "...love covers a multitude of sins." (I Pet.
4:8). This is how God's love is demonstrated through everyday people.
Practicing this will also develop your integrity and trustworthiness.

BEFORE YOU BEGIN
THE CHALLENGE

PRAYER: HOW AND WHEN?

Without prayer, we are empty and our relationship with God is a sham.

Imagine a marriage where the husband and wife never sit down to talk. They work. They eat. They sleep. Zero communication. While roommates can do that much, a healthy and happy marriage calls for more!

I can remember a period of my marriage when my husband and I were too busy to date. All of our energy went into the business of life and the church. All of the communicating we did *before* marriage used to soak up hours of our day. So what happened? We forgot to *stay connected to the reason* we married in the first place! We married for the bliss of our conversation, our tenderness, and the way we found humor in weird places. We *made time* before marriage, but let it slip after we said, "I do." We had to be honest with ourselves and one another to get back on track.

We all do the same thing with our faith. We get busy with life, politics, and work, and we forget the joy of our personal connection with Christ! There is no one greater to have in your corner through life. Only He can speak to you the way He does. And guess what? Busy as you are, you have the time for more of Him.

That, my friend, is how you begin to discover who Jesus truly is on a personal level.

HOW SHOULD YOU PRAY?

There are so many types of prayer! During the challenge, you should stretch yourself and try new forms of prayer. The variety alone helps to keep your mind engaged in the process. I'll list a few ways to get you started:

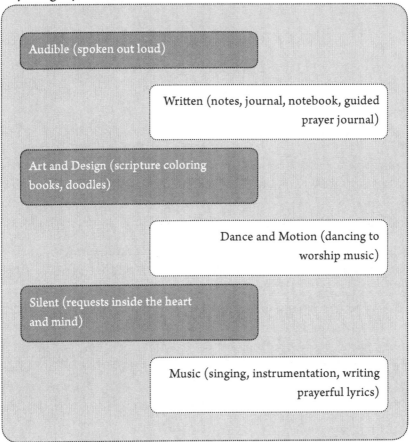

Audible (spoken out loud)

Written (notes, journal, notebook, guided prayer journal)

Art and Design (scripture coloring books, doodles)

Dance and Motion (dancing to worship music)

Silent (requests inside the heart and mind)

Music (singing, instrumentation, writing prayerful lyrics)

> Planned Private Location (closet, room, special quiet area)
>
> Spontaneous (on-the-spot talks with God)

WHEN SHOULD YOU PRAY?

The best time of day for prayer is whatever time you most naturally can make for it. When can you be alert and focused on speaking and then listening for a few minutes? I like to pray most while I clean or exercise. It kills two birds with one stone, and when I'm finished, I feel accomplished. I know that I didn't just "clock in" with God. I really laid out my heart to Him while I was active. Try scheduling a few minutes of prayer at different times of the day to see what works best for you.

HOW CAN SCRIPTURE BE USED TO HELP YOU PRAY?

One morning, before I went for a run, I realized that I didn't want to listen to music that day. I had a list of verses that I had written down regarding a certain need in my life that I wanted to review, but time wasn't on my side. I grabbed my cell phone, opened up the voice recorder, and began reading the verses to myself, putting emphasis where I needed it. That day, when I ran, I didn't need music—I listened to myself reading those verses again and again. It was weird at first hearing my own voice. But after a few minutes, I could really focus on the message of the scriptures and how they applied to my life.

On a different day, I gathered and wrote my verses down, but I couldn't pray. I didn't know where to start! So I took my time and read each verse out loud, and then I paraphrased it in a way that fit my situation. For example:

Colossians 4:2 says, "Devote yourselves to prayer, being watchful and thankful."

So when I prayed, I paraphrased it saying:

> *Lord, Your Word in **Colossians 4 encourages me to devote myself to prayer**. Help me to focus on You, giving our relationship the time it needs to grow. **Help me to be watchful** of my surroundings and what I'm involving myself in today. And **help me to remain thankful in all things**, even when it seems like they don't go my way. Your plans are perfect, and I need You.*

Boom. Done.

Do you see how simple that was?

Psalm 119:105 tells us that God's Word is a lamp for our feet and a light for our path. I mention this because we don't know how to pray at times, but the Spirit helps us through Scripture. When you begin to look up verses that apply to specific circumstances, you can read them out loud and pray them directly, adding names and emphasis of your own. For example:

II Timothy 1:7 says, "For God has not given us a spirit of fear and timidity, but of power, love, and self-discipline."

Using this verse in prayer, I might say, *"Lord, Your Word says that You have not given me a spirit of fear and timidity, but of power, love and self-discipline. Help me to trust You more and believe the promises made to me."*

You can also personalize Scriptures as you write your prayers like this:

"Be determined and confident. Do not be afraid of them. Your God, the Lord Himself, will be with you. He will not fail you or abandon you." (Deut. 31:6 GNT)

Prayer: (Insert your name), be determined and confident. Do not be afraid of them. God, the Lord Himself, will be with you. He will not fail you or abandon you.

Doing this will always remind you what God says about a matter. Then take a few seconds for quiet reflection on the verses you prayed with. Where do you feel challenged? Where do you feel encouraged? Where do you sense His direction? Make note of these moments and then move on with your day. This is how you reconnect with the thoughts of God.

The point of prayer is connecting, not just talking about problems. There is nothing worse than a conversation with someone who doesn't listen while you speak, but instead spends the time preparing his or her next point. Go to God in prayer, and be sincere. You be *you*, and let God be *God*. Talk and listen. Rinse and repeat.

Challenge Dates ___/ ___/ ___ *to* ___/ ___/ ___

PREP DAY

My Partner:

I Will Fast From:

I Will Avoid This Type of Media:

I Will Replace the Time With:

I Will Listen To:

I Will Read:

CHALLENGE DAY 1
THE DISCONNECT

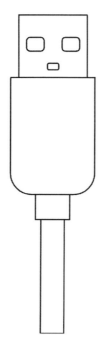

DAY I

Challenge: *Create a special place for prayer in your home. Keep it simple.*

How?

> *Consider your space and how you can make it your own for prayer.*
> *You will need at least: a Bible, a notebook, and something to write with.*
> *Search the web for ideas, using key phrases like: how to create a prayer room, prayer closet, prayer caddy, and quiet corner.*
> *Schedule a daily call time with your Prayer Partner (just about fifteen minutes).*

Reminders

- Prioritize change.
- Proactively refuse to disconnect from God for these seven days.
- Call or meet with your accountability partner at a set time each day (it can be different according to your schedules). ***Do not text as a check-in* for these seven days.**
- Discuss the challenge of the day and how it affected you personally. **Pray for one another before hanging up. Nothing long!**
- Hold each other accountable for each day's challenge—no excuses!
- Discuss today's challenge and reading before praying together.

DAY I

Spaces I Can Use for Prayer: *(e.g. a favorite chair, an empty office, a porch, or a vehicle while you are on a break)*

Moments I Can Use for Prayer: *(e.g. use a lunch break or a train ride, give up a television show or thirty minutes of online time)*

Prayer: *"God, help me learn to focus on You. Forgive me of every wrong and help me to let go of every negative weight. Give strength and hope to those around me through the peace You share with me in our times together this week."*

© Concetta Green, 2017

DAY 1 READING
THE DISCONNECT

For many of us in the digital age, there is nothing better than having access to Wi-Fi. The internet provides convenient and instant access to anything you want. And when you need to get online, there is nothing more frustrating than seeing a list of Wi-Fi networks that you can't connect to, particularly when one of those accounts already belongs to you. You may take time to troubleshoot it or try a work-around using a different device. But the inability to connect where you *should* be able to will irritate you until it's fixed.

There is a similar disconnect happening spiritually for a lot of us. That same discomfort of being locked out of a network is what Christians feel when they can't pray. But also it feels like too much effort to fix it.

We don't want to pray.

I mean, we *want* to pray, but how long is it going to take to get connected? And once we're there, will we find what we need?

Starting now, I want you to begin to view prayer as your free connection to God Himself. You have full access. Prayer is like a secret meeting room for you and the Creator of heaven and earth. It's a big deal. And that place of connection can be flexible and engaging. After you accept Christ as your Savior, there is a daily decision that is made about your relationship with Him. You decide passively or actively each moment whether or not to remain intimately connected with His heart and mind.

But what about the seasons when you find yourself having drifted very far from this relationship somehow? How do you handle the disconnect? I think it's important to begin with two questions:

1. Why am I choosing to stay disconnected from God?

2. What am I avoiding?

Give these questions a moment in your mind, and write down some possible answers here:

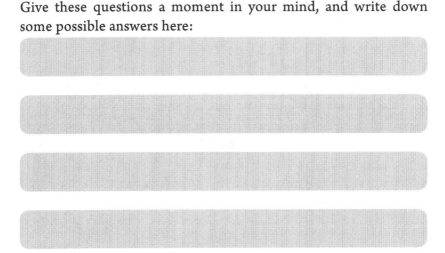

The New Testament tells us that Jesus would withdraw often and pray: "...Jesus often withdrew to lonely places and prayed" (Luke 5:16).

In this verse, we see Christ setting the example of actively choosing to disconnect from the world in exchange for times of connection with God the Father. This habit shows us that Jesus prioritized the time spent in conversation with God, actively sharing His heart and receiving instruction.

When we choose to regularly unplug from our intimacy with Christ, we go somewhere else instead. Where do you go? When you are not in the secret place of prayer with Him, where can the core of who you are be found hiding? Think about this for a moment:

If the verse were written about you today, what would it say?

_____ often withdrew to _____ and _____

(insert your name)

If the Son of God needed a secret place, then we *all* need a secret place (Ps. 91). I looked further in the Scriptures and was reminded that: "The name of the LORD is a fortified tower; the righteous *run to it* and are safe" (Prov. 18:10, emphasis mine).

For the believer, where we hide ourselves is crucial. Any hiding place beyond the shadow of the Almighty won't provide the depth of security we all need. You need the strength and protection that is found in Him.

Don't disconnect. Find your secret place of prayer. Go there often.

DAY 1 THOUGHTS

CHALLENGE DAY 2
PRAYING WITH FOCUS

The work during day two is important and may require an additional thirty minutes to find verses and create the cards you prefer. See the resources listed on page 73.

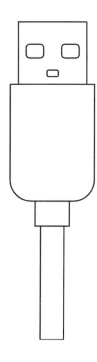

DAY 2

Challenge: Create seven flashcards with scriptures that inspire you to pray. Post them in your new prayer space.

How?

> Search online for Bible verses that hold meaning for your needs. If you don't have internet access, use a basic Bible concordance to look up topical verses. Post the cards where you'll see them most. Write them down by hand on the next page first.

> **Unsure?** Search Google for ideas, using a key phrase like "How to make Scripture flashcards for prayer."

> **Limited space?** Tape the cards or notes inside your journal or small notebook.

> **Prefer digital?** You can also save images of the verses or verse memes to scroll through on your device. This is a helpful alternative next time you're tempted to visit social media this week.

Reminders

- Prioritize change.
- Proactively refuse to disconnect from God for these seven days.
- Call or meet with your accountability partner at a set time each day (it can be different according to your schedules). *Do not text as a check-in* for these seven days.
- Discuss the challenge of the day and how it affected you personally. **Pray for one another before hanging up. Nothing long!**
- Hold each other accountable for each day's challenge—no excuses!

DAY 2

Seven verses that inspire me to pray:

DAY 2

REFLECT: *How Did This Part of the Challenge Affect Me Today?*

Prayer: *"God, I thank You that I can find encouragement in Your Word to pray. Help me to recognize distractions and time wasters in my life. I want to rest on Your promises and find an undercurrent of joy each time I look to You."*

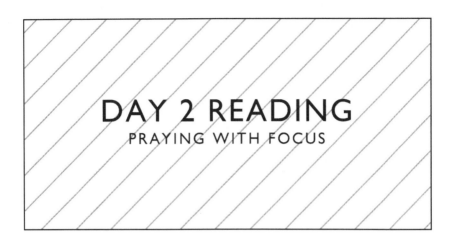

DAY 2 READING
PRAYING WITH FOCUS

T HE crosshair image is powerful to me. This simple circle with lines is what sharpshooters see inside of their long-distance scope to help lock in on their mark. When I realized that personal prayers needed focus to guide them, I opened a notebook and sketched one out to look like this:

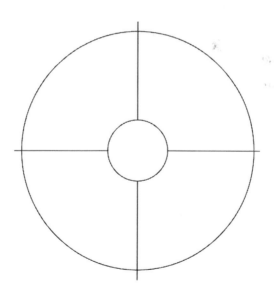

I put my prayer request at the center of the crosshairs and wondered how God felt about my request in the grand scheme of things. So, I took the main concern, which at the time was fear, and did an online search for Bible verses about fear. I wrote down the verses that seemed to encourage my heart and tell me how God viewed fear. I ended up filling the blank space surrounding my prayer request, and it looked a lot like this:

My Prayer Focus

1. Praise

I bless You for sharing glimpses of her future. Thanks for her destiny that shifts the Kingdom of God and this world for YOU. Thank You for the souls saved through her life and witness.

3. Introspection

Father, Karen is Yours. Let Your will be made clear for her and help us align with heaven & not fight Your desires. Your will, not mine!

Behold, I give you a wise and discerning mind, so that none like you has been before you and none like you shall arise after you. (I Kings 3:12 ESV)

For we are his workmanship, created in Christ Jesus for good works, which God prepared beforehand, that we should walk in them. (Ephesians 2:10 ESV)

You are my hiding place; you will protect me from trouble and surround me with songs of deliverance. (Psalm 32:7–8)

Mentoring Karen (my niece) through fear

My Presence will go with you, and I will gove you rest. (Exodus 33:14)

I sought the LORD, and he answered me; delivered me from all my fears. (Psalm 34:4)

2. Forgiveness

Help me not to serve my niece in pride or selfishness. Thank You that I am free from the past. Thank You for new wisdom to guide her into her future!

4. Gratitude

Thank You that Karen is fearfully and wonderfully made. Crafted for Your purpose and destiny. Thank You for good, sound friendships and loves in her life! Strong identity and witness for you, oh God!

Thoughts after Prayer & the Word

I have been more patient with Karen's personality. Her confidence has started to turn around.

By the time I was finished, my need seemed very small and God's concern for me seemed very big. Looking again at the shape and the lines reminded me that prayer is the meeting point between heaven (the vertical line) and earth (the horizontal line). Prayer is the space where we invite God's Kingdom to come and His will to be done here on earth. I invite you to try this format of finding verses that connect with your life and visually making them stand out. You will find blank versions of this template for future use on page 79.

Once you have a few scriptures to target the need at the center of your Focused Prayer Sheet, there are a few important moments to take in your prayer time:

1. *Praise*

   It's important to begin any time of prayer with thanks to God. Celebrate who He is and what He has already done in praise. Push yourself to spend time being thankful to Him. This is also a great moment to sing or play songs of praise to get yourself started (Ps. 100, Ps. 34:1–7).

2. *Forgiveness*

   After a time of thanks, ask the Lord for forgiveness of sins that you are aware of and not aware of. While finding verses for prayer, you may have seen areas in your heart and mind where your motives have not been the best. You may also be holding a grudge that needs to be released. This is the space to ask God for help to let those things go and receive His grace. It may not happen instantly, but keep asking (Mt. 6:12–15, Ps. 51).

3. *Introspection*

   Take a moment to look within. We usually believe we know what the perfect solution to our problems would be. As you pull scriptures into your prayer life, let them remind you that we are always asking for *God's* will to be done. In prayer, I would like you to give God room to prove what is the best outcome. Remember, His perspective is wide and detailed and working for your good. Ask Him to provide what you and the situation most need (Rom. 8:28, Isa. 55:9, Mt. 6:9–11).

This is a great space to pray for the need at the center of your target. Pray for it using the verses you have surrounding the issue. Declare God's promises over the matter.

4. *Gratitude*

Thank God in advance for His desired outcome. When an issue comes to your attention, God is trusting you to bring it back to Him in prayer. The end of your prayer time should be a return of that trust. It is here where you stop asking for anything and you exalt God only. Think of His goodness, remember His grace, and thank Him for it all. Tell Him how amazing He is to you. Consider ending in silence, enjoying God's peace. After prayer, write about how you feel regarding the situation now that you have explored what God's Word had to say (Ps. 116:1, Ps. 26:8, Ps. 95:6).

SPECIAL NOTE

You will only develop the discipline of prayer by adding structure to your time. I don't expect you to use the Prayer Focus Sheet every time you pray. This is a guide to walk you through the process of praying the Word and adding creativity that has been missing. Use the printed version in the book, make a list in your journal, or use a poster board; whatever you do, just start praying!

CHALLENGE DAY 3
WHEN YOU DON'T HAVE TIME

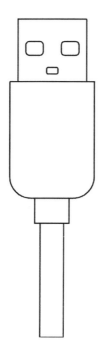

DAY 3

Challenge: *Create a list of ten specific things or people to pray for.*

How?

> *BE SPECIFIC*
> *Use pictures, names, and phrases that remind you what to pray for.*
> *On today's call with your Challenge Partner, each of you must share one need from your list and then pray for one another in those areas.*

Reminders

- Prioritize change.
- Proactively refuse to disconnect from God for these seven days.
- Call or meet with your accountability partner at a set time each day (it can be different according to your schedules). **Do not text as a check-in for these seven days.**
- Discuss the challenge of the day and how it affected you personally. **Pray for one another before hanging up. Nothing long!**
- Hold each other accountable for each day's challenge—no excuses!

DAY 3

My "Top 10" right now:

_____

_____

_____

_____

_____

_____

_____

_____

_____

My Partner's Prayer Request Today:

_____

DAY 3

REFLECT: *How did you feel during today's challenge? What did you go through while making your list?*

DAY 3 READING
WHEN YOU DON'T HAVE TIME

D o you ever feel that the word *busy* never adequately describes everything on your to-do list? Do you feel that it's easier for you to help other people do what they want than it is for you to carve out a slice of time to help yourself? Somehow your personal desires seem insurmountable, but helping someone else is easy. It just takes a little time to care, right? But at the end of the day, once you have helped everyone, you are left feeling alone and empty, wondering why no one is willing to help you dig deep to accomplish the things in your heart. In moments like this, time can seem to be *against* you because you have so little left for yourself. How does this happen?

Well, my friend, your time is like money. And when it's not valued enough to be budgeted properly, everyone feels they have a right to it. Except for you. Without a plan that tells each hour where to go, your time will get lost in work, last-minute emergencies, or hours online that have nothing to do with your true goals.

If you find yourself dissatisfied with the lack of progress in your spiritual life, it is likely that you have not set any goals in that area. Your time has not been prioritized to help you mature spiritually and deepen your connection with God. When was the last time you made an appointment with yourself to write down your personal goals with a list of specific actions, dates, times, and resources to make them happen? Or have you been waiting for a hero to come and drag your purpose out of you? We sometimes put silent expectations on people around us to force us to do what is right. Quietly, we hold them accountable for how we decide to use our time. We long for a spouse, a pastor, or a mentor to see our greatness and be the hero that pulls us kicking and screaming toward destiny.

Do you see how ridiculous that perspective is once you lay it out on paper?

Here on earth, we are individually responsible for our time because the hero we need has already come. As Christians, that hero is Christ within you, and He has put inside of you the exact same power that raised Him from the dead (Rom. 8:11, *The Message*)! That very strength is accessible by sharing your most precious gift of time with God. In your moments with Him, the Holy Spirit can recharge the dreams you are hiding with new life. He desires to help you put first things first. And the Word of God provides the courage you need to do the work and complete the tasks ahead.

Dear friend, if you are alive, then you do have time. Value it enough to make plans with it. This prayer challenge is the first step to learning how to budget your time the same way you budget any other resource. The goal is to have some spiritual growth and success that translates into other areas of your life. But it starts with recognizing the true hero and you planning time to connect with Him.

CHALLENGE DAY 4
CONNECTING WITH GOD AND PEOPLE

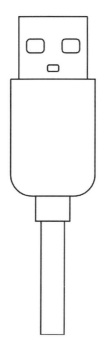

DAY 4

Challenge: Take a prayer walk for fifteen minutes. Pray for three of the needs from your top ten list.

How?

> *Get moving! Use the time to de-stress and discuss the needs with God.*

> *Ideas: Walk around the block or exercise while quietly seeking God with fervor and intensity.*

Reminders

- Prioritize change.

- Proactively refuse to disconnect from God for these seven days.

- Call or meet with your accountability partner at a set time each day (it can be different according to your schedules). **Do not text as a check-in for these seven days.**

- Discuss the challenge of the day and how it affected you personally. **Pray for one another before hanging up. Nothing long!**

- Hold each other accountable for each day's challenge—no excuses!

DAY 4

Today's three needs:

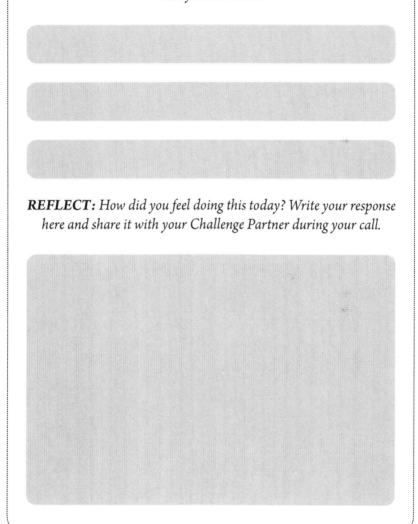

REFLECT: *How did you feel doing this today? Write your response here and share it with your Challenge Partner during your call.*

DAY 4 READING
CONNECTING WITH GOD AND PEOPLE

HAVING a conversation with God while you walk is a great way to reconnect with Him. Imagine Him walking beside you and begin telling Him what's on your mind. Take pauses between topics to listen quietly. The Holy Spirit may remind you of verses that address your needs or you may simply sense the Lord listening. Personal visits like this with the Lord are fulfilling and special. They teach you how to enjoy being with Him while keeping an open heart. When you pray with your partner later today, you may find yourself more comfortable with quiet moments because you have practiced it privately.

I realize that praying out loud with a partner may be new for you. If you flub a word or feel stuck, learn to laugh with your partner and move on. Pray what you mean to say without getting lost in religious jargon or elaborate phrases. Just talk, petitioning God using Scripture and your regular style of speaking. What matters most is that you bring your full self to the moment of prayer. If you desire authentic connection in your relationships, then both of you must be vulnerable. Just remember: you're trying something new, so it takes awhile to feel totally comfortable!

In times of prayer, it is also common to temporarily share the emotional experience of those you are interceding for. You may pray about something and find yourself overcome with emotion. This is heaven's way of giving you empathy for the matter, as if the feelings were your own. Don't hide from the feelings, and don't hold them beyond your times of prayer. Express what the emotions are, and ask God to share His peace with you and those you are praying for. Let the Word of God speak to those feelings and strengthen you as you pray so that you can rise from prayer, feeling lifted and not burdened. The Word of God and His Holy Spirit must do the heavy work, and all you have to do is open up and connect with Him.

CHALLENGE DAY 5

EXPOSING YOUR BIAS

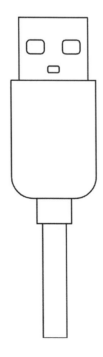

DAY 5

Challenge: In your special place of prayer, turn off distractions and write out your personal prayers to God on the next page.

How?

> Write a prayer for three more needs from your "Top 10" list.

> Add a written prayer for those affected by a major news story from today. Ask God for greater compassion for people who are not like you.

Reminders

- Prioritize change.
- Proactively refuse to disconnect from God for these seven days.
- Call or meet with your accountability partner at a set time each day (it can be different according to your schedules). *Do not text as a check-in* **for these seven days.**
- Discuss the challenge of the day and how it affected you personally. **Pray for one another before hanging up. Nothing long!**
- Hold each other accountable for each day's challenge—no excuses!

DAY 5

Written prayer for three needs:

Written prayer for a news story:

DAY 5

REFLECT: *What have you begun to notice about yourself when it comes to prayer (good and bad)? Write it down here and share it with your Challenge Partner today.*

DAY 5 READING
EXPOSING YOUR BIAS

Ah, bias. We all have it. This idea came into my life through a management course I took during my master's program. It changed me forever. I learned that every person holds ideas about the world based on any number of factors and that his or her perspective is ultimately manifested in various behaviors, consciously and subconsciously.

Bias can color what you see because the assumptions of your mind create a backstory when no words have even been spoken.

The foolish person says, "I have zero bias."

The wise person says, "I have bias and pray for grace to look beyond myself to see what is truly before me."

I want you to ask God to expose and remove bias in your prayer life. Why? Because the way bias shapes our beliefs about solutions applies to our own life and the lives of others. Bias is the lens through which we view everything. It colors what we see. In prayer, I want you to release your image of what you believe to be the solution to your problem. I want you to first make room for God's answer. Ask for it. Look for it. He will allow you to find it (Matt. 7:7–12). On our own, we have a tendency to make superficial judgment calls. Those calls are often based on our own limited perception, and they taint our thoughts and interactions going forward.

It's time to learn how to step out of your perspective (which is fairly one-sided) and pursue the heart of God. Challenge your inner assumptions with an open heart when you talk to Him. You might find a new perspective waiting for you!

I befriended a dad once whose life choices kept his child in various forms of distress. When I heard updates that were troubling to me, I could never pray about it and walk away in peace. One day, I clearly heard the Lord speak to my heart. The thought read clear across my head like a ticker tape: "You get upset about that family because you relate to the child's experience. You've felt powerless as a young girl, and you think the child does, too."

Welp! The old southern saying goes: "The hit dog will holler." I sure wanted to holler in that moment.

The issues from my past made it difficult for me to pray with ease for that particular family. In that moment, I repented. I asked the Lord to heal my heart and help me to forgive my own past and move on. God was in control, not me. Adopting that position of humility in my heart made it *so* much easier to pray for that family. I found verses that spoke to wholeness to guide my prayers for them. And my own hang-ups were finally out of the way in that situation.

Now, I'm sure this sounds super easy, but it wasn't! It was uncomfortable to face my own weakness, but the Lord brought healing to my heart privately while I prayed for the healing of others. That is one of the less-celebrated benefits of prayer. In that private place, moments of unexpected clarity occur when you can have an open-ended approach to your personal time with God.

As you become more aware of God, your inner issues will surface. Identify them, being specific about the emotions that arise. Write them down, and talk with Him about them. You must be clear so that you don't confuse your issues with the needs of others. When you reach a point where you feel unsure, speak with your pastor, a counselor, or a mature Christian friend for direction. Wisdom is knowing when you've reached the limit of your own understanding and beginning to trust the Lord for help (Prov. 15:22, Prov. 9:10, Prov. 1:7)!

SPECIAL NOTE

Ask the Lord to show you your own biases. Then ask the Lord to help you see situations with His perspective.

CHALLENGE DAY 6
GOSSIP

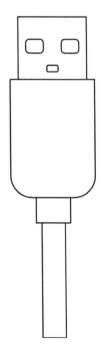

DAY 6

Challenge: *In your special place of prayer, turn off distractions and fill out a Focused Prayer Sheet for three more of your "Top 10" requests.*

How?

> Even if you're not artistic, make the verses vibrant to you.
> Ask the Lord to speak to your heart as you draw/write/color.
> Use your Focused Prayer Sheets during tonight's prayer session with your Challenge Partner. Pray for your own needs using the verses you found.
> Keep the sheets private.

Reminders

- Prioritize change.
- Proactively refuse to disconnect from God for these seven days.
- Call or meet with your accountability partner at a set time each day (it can be different according to your schedules). *Do not text as a check-in* **for these seven days.**
- Discuss the challenge of the day and how it affected you personally. **Pray for one another before hanging up. Nothing long!**
- Hold each other accountable for each day's challenge—no excuses!

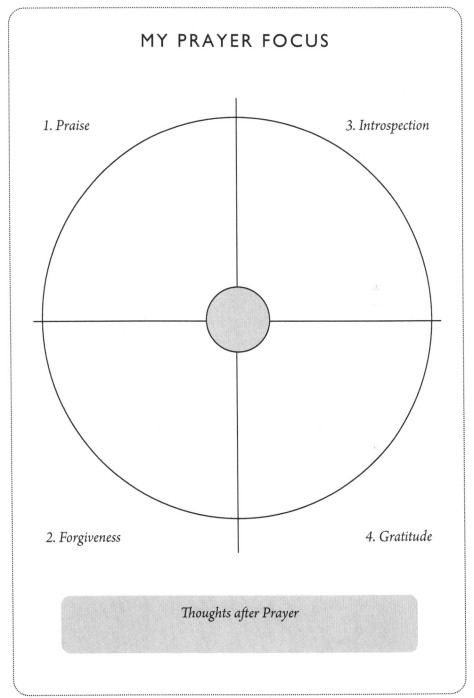

MY PRAYER FOCUS

1. Praise

3. Introspection

2. Forgiveness

4. Gratitude

Thoughts after Prayer

Focused Prayer Sheet © Concetta Green, 2017

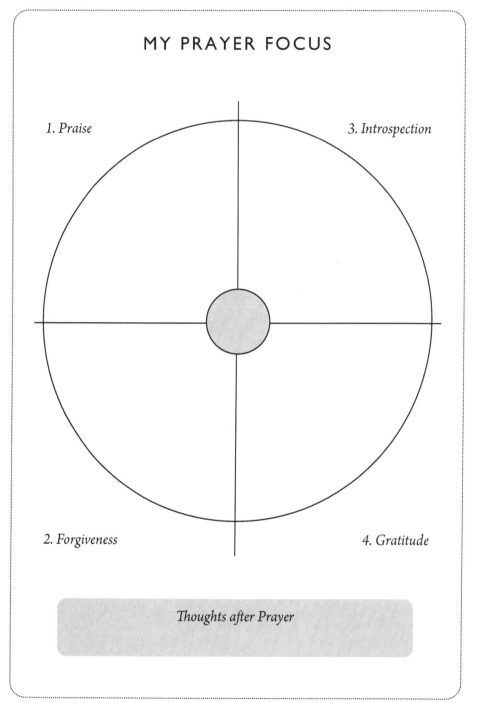

MY PRAYER FOCUS

1. Praise

3. Introspection

2. Forgiveness

4. Gratitude

Thoughts after Prayer

Focused Prayer Sheet © Concetta Green, 2017

MY PRAYER FOCUS

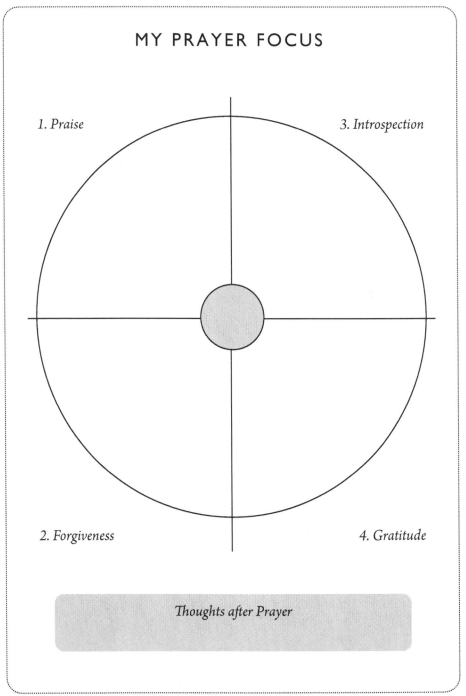

1. Praise

3. Introspection

2. Forgiveness

4. Gratitude

Thoughts after Prayer

Focused Prayer Sheet © Concetta Green, 2017

DAY 6 READING
GOSSIP

"A gossip betrays a confidence; so avoid anyone who talks too much" (Prov. 20:19).

Do you trade secrets to look better to someone you want to impress or to gain access to a group of people? Or can God trust you with confidential information? If private details about other people's lives always come to you (unsolicited), it could be a sign that God wants you to pray about those things and not just talk about them with anyone who will listen.

God may be trying to ensure that your heart is steeped in compassion and empathy. He doesn't care about the latest scoop.

Remember how we saw Jesus going off to pray in private? We never heard of Him publicly blabbing on and on about His prayers for each person. He only shared those details at certain times among certain groups. We see this shortly before Jesus was betrayed by his disciples. Over dinner with them, He says to the one named Simon (also called Peter), "Simon, I've prayed for you in particular that you not give in or give out" (Luke 22:31–32, *The Message*). Jesus said this privately, not as part of His public sermon. He waited for a private moment to speak directly to someone he cared about. Jesus knew that Simon was about to betray Him, but He didn't want Simon to let that failure make him quit. Jesus prayed for Simon while alone and then later shared a portion of what His prayer was to encourage him. This moment is a beautiful example of discipline and confidentiality in prayer.

Spending time in the presence of God should change you and draw you to maturity. The way that Jesus encouraged Simon not to quit after a huge mistake is the same way Jesus speaks to us today. Your personal time with Him should be encouraging because you learn God's voice through studying Scripture. Time spent soaking in God's promises naturally deepens your faith. And deeper faith affects your behavior and how you interact with people.

That thought always excites me. If I am truly spending time with God, parts of me will change. Not in some freakish way that makes me a robot. But my truest self always shines through because, in our conversations, God helps me throw away the junk habits, like gossip, that I don't need. When I leave His presence, my smile is brighter and no one else knows why. It's in my place of prayer that all of my secrets are known and safe!

In your time of new growth in God, begin to treat the secrets of others the way you would like your own secrets handled. Would you want the latest news about you to spread? Become the final stop when the issues of others are being traded back and forth. Pray for the person and the private matter, asking God to intervene and bring help.

Can you see how all of this begins to let God change your heart and the focus of your prayers?

You can now more easily recognize the mature Christians versus those who are stuck; look for the ones still growing in love and grace. Look for the ones who speak louder with actions than their voices. Look for those who remain humble and patient; they are still weeping for the lost and broken. These are people who pray with focus to know God, to seek His will (heaven's answers to earth's needs), and to keep an open and yielding heart.

If you don't see any of those types of believers around, then find a mirror. Become the person you desire to see. Without saying a word, your discipline to pray privately will manifest outwardly when you don't even realize it. It will bless everyone who comes into contact with you.

CHALLENGE DAY 7
NOT PERFECT

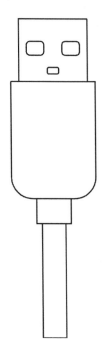

DAY 7

Challenge: In your place of prayer, turn off distractions and write your own psalm to the Lord.

How?

> *Give fresh thanks to God for what He has done in* **your life**, *who He is to you, and who you want Him to be. Give it a title (see the book of Psalms for examples).*

> *After that, take a moment on your knees to pray out loud for the final request on your "Top 10" list. Speak to God about the need as if you were talking to a friend who had the power to change things (because He does have that power).*

> *Share your personal psalm with your Challenge Partner over the phone—don't be shy!*

Reminders

- Prioritize change.
- Proactively refuse to disconnect from God for these seven days.
- Call or meet with your accountability partner at a set time each day (it can be different according to your schedules). **Do not text as a check-in for these seven days.**
- Discuss the challenge of the day and how it affected you personally. **Pray for one another before hanging up. Nothing long!**
- Hold each other accountable for each day's challenge—no excuses!

DAY 7

My Psalm Title:

DAY 7

REFLECT: *Was it odd praying out loud today in such a regular way? How did it feel to write your own psalm to the Lord?*

DAY 7

LAST-CALL DISCUSSION POINTS:

What have I learned about myself this week?

What have I learned about you?

Where have I been blaming others for my difficulties?

Where do I find the most joy and peace?

What have I learned about God and prayer this week?

DAY 7

Now that the prayer challenge is complete, stay connected to your Challenge Partner with encouraging texts and calls when you think of them!

Consider setting up a time to reconnect for prayer regularly (e.g. once a week, once a month, or in three months for another seven days of prayer).

Prioritize change by keeping at least one fifteen-minute window open for personal prayer each day. Schedule it in your phone or calendar, and keep it fresh and personal!

DAY 7 READING
NOT PERFECT

According to Romans 3, none of us are perfect. So can we just let that idea go? Expect other Christians to be just as flawed and human as you are. I believe the quiet longing within us to achieve perfection is our eternal spirit craving for what only God can offer. Since we are wrapped in flesh, we tend to search for perfection here on earth in partners, celebrities, and leaders. Although we commonly declare that nobody's perfect, we are still sorely disappointed each time someone's behavior proves this to be true.

Our lack of perfection in Christian relationships can be tempered through accountability. Having to answer to someone makes you think twice and remember the ripple effect of your decision-making. When I wanted to get physically fit, I consulted a personal trainer. I didn't realize that the trainer cared about what I ate around the clock and how I treated my body. The trainer became someone I had to answer to for my decisions. I felt shy about sharing so much, but having to check in helped to make sure I met my goals. I am not sure why we are so willing to treat our spiritual side differently. Many of us feel embarrassed about what we don't know, and those feelings cause us to become guarded with the community we are supposed to feel at home with.

If you are not careful, the convenience of social media will make you feel as if the internet is the safest place to vent. It isn't. Because we spend so much time staring at the same pictures of the same people online, it is easy to feel a common bond with them. However, everything online is superficial and generally one-sided. The internet is not the safest place for your heart. It keeps a record of your wrongs (I Cor. 13:4–7). Rely instead on the people who know you in person. That is how you build your own community.

Take time to develop relationships that are stable and worthy of your trust. If the people are full of grace, they will not reject or ridicule you. They will support you and point you to God's truth, even when you don't like what is being said. In healthy relationships, being challenged to grow is a sign that you are loved enough for them to take the risk of telling you a difficult truth and vice versa (Prov. 27:6, Prov. 3:11–12).

Let me ease your mind. Every Christian on this earth is trusting God to help with their flaws. It is a comfort to connect with someone on a personal level who shares your faith. You should be able to share experiences and insights in a safe environment rooted in God's love. Don't let fear cause you to keep other Christians, especially your challenge partner, at arm's length emotionally. To our detriment, that habit causes us to manage our relationship with God the same way. The Lord created us for relationships and to connect with Him and with others (Eccl. 4:9–12). Don't cheat yourself and your world out of that blessing. Be your authentic self and allow others to do the same, knowing that no one is perfect, but, together, we are stronger than when we are alone.

NOW THAT YOU'RE PRAYING AGAIN...

THE insights shared with you in the preceding chapters are meant to give you some direction as you revamp your prayer life. Try incorporating the ideas, and you will find that your thoughts become clearer. Why? Because you are intentionally slowing down to focus and give your prayer time purpose. The renewed discipline will shift your subconscious attitude and reshape your current outlook.

When you pray, what will you "zero in on" to keep your brain *off* of autopilot? What scriptures will you write and review to remind yourself of how God sees the situation? The Focused Prayer Sheet is designed to help you develop the habit of connecting scripture to real life through prayer. It is meant to help you stay mentally present when you come into contact with the Word. When I research verses that relate to a certain topic in my life, I keep those that strike my heart. When reading the verses aloud, try changing the pronouns to make them fit you personally. Our names may not appear in the pages, but we are included in any place where the Lord is speaking to His people or His church.

Identify where you are wasting time and choosing to disconnect. Set goals for your spiritual life that you can be accountable for. Stay alert so that you *can* pray clearly. When you feel something trying to block you from prayer, show up anyway and use the Word and worship to connect with your heavenly Father.

A FOCUSED PRAYER LIFE GIVES YOU MORE:

Flexibility

Character

Integrity

Compassion

Emotional Intelligence

Discernment

Patience and Awareness of Proper Timing

Endurance

Discipline

Personal Healing

YOU SHOULD EMERGE FROM PRAYER:

Feeling Connected

At Peace

Determined

Encouraged

Focused

Challenged

Refreshed

Cherish your connection with God and chase after it always. Don't worry about becoming "too deep" and "getting lost" in weird mysticism here. Get in touch with your Creator so that you can function at maximum capacity and get some joy in your life! The only time wasted is the time you spend in distraction. Prayer should offer a fresh moment with God each day. The forces of this world are designed to make you disconnect from Him. I challenge you: don't let those forces win.

The next time you reach another stale place in your spiritual walk, **you will know how to connect with God.** With or without a partner, you will remember the tools and strategies in this book and find your way.

RESOURCES

BIBLE WEBSITES & APPS

BibleGateway.com

*This website and free app provides easy access to multiple translations of the Bible. You can also sign up for daily devotional emails. In addition, Bible Gateway has an audio Bible feature for those who prefer to listen to Scripture. The **Streetlights Bible App** by GRIP Outreach for Youth is a fantastic audio Bible and more for hip-hop lovers. Also, **The Bible App by YouVersion** is a rich resource full of Bible translations, devotionals, scripture memes, and daily readings.*

MUSIC WEBSITES & APPS

Pandora.com or Spotify.com

*These two apps allow you to stream free worship music of any style. You can create your own playlists or listen to suggested songs. This is a great way to explore a variety of Christian artists. Worship music keeps the heart and mind soaked in thoughts that are aligned with God's Word. Purchasing subscriptions is not required for either service. **Amazon Music** always offers free listening to Prime Members for select Gospel albums, and **Apple Music** is a no-brainer for die-hard Apple fans.*

DIGITAL CALENDARS & ALARMS

*The calendar and/or alarm clock setting on your personal device can provide useful reminders for your daily prayer times. Give the alarm setting a special name to remind yourself to unplug, pray alone, and connect with your Challenge Partner. And whatever you do, don't hit "Snooze!" You can also try the **Echo Prayer App** which offers shared prayer requests and personal reminders.*

DIGITAL VOICE MEMOS

Most modern devices come preloaded with a voice memo feature to record short reminders. If you don't like writing, try using this feature to remember items to pray for. If you have a list of scriptures that you want to remember, you can also record yourself or a friend reading them and listen to it later.

TIME MANAGEMENT APPS

Moment Time Tracker App

*This free app tracks how often you use your phone each day. It can help you set daily screen time limits. There is a paid upgrade that provides additional functions. **The Freedom App**, which is the basic version of this app, is free for a few tries. It allows you to block the use of certain apps on your phone for set periods of time during the day with the goal of increasing your productivity. Both apps are excellent tools to measure your actual phone useage.*

CHRISTIAN LIFESTYLE RESOURCES

***YouTube.com** and **Podcasts** are fantastic tools for accessing free sermons, interviews, and music from your favorite ministries and Christian content providers. Encouraging podcasts can be listened to at your convenience on any computer or smart device. The **Sprinkle of Jesus App** and **SprinkleofJesus.com** provide a wealth of resources for believers looking to add more faith to their daily walk.*

CREATIVE RESOURCES
ART SUPPLIES

*There is no need to spend a lot of money on journals, highlighters, index cards, fancy pens, or sticky notes. Try a Dollar Tree or a craft store first. Great for visual learners, **Pinterest.com** is filled with pictures and well-designed printables on prayer time and almost every aspect of Christian living. It is free and very easy to use.*

A PHYSICAL BIBLE

*Never underestimate the power of an actual **Bible** in your hand. Apps are convenient to listen to the Bible or read on the go, but when it's time to sit down and study, nothing is better than marking up your own paper Bible with colorful notes inside. Review a few common translations online to find one that is easiest for you to understand (the New International Version, The Amplified Bible, The Message, the Holy Bible, and New Living Translation are all easy to understand). Then purchase a physical Bible in your favorite translation. Fill the margins of it with your comments and reactions to the verses. Highlighting the words helps them stick in your mind. You can even have your Bible cover tricked out by an artist like **Chris Errington @TheHipsterHousewife**. Bibles can be purchased at bookstores or online at websites like **Amazon.com, WalMart.com, ChristianBook.com**, and **Lifeway.com** to name a few.*

A DEVOTIONAL

*Using a daily devotional helps to give your prayer time direction. There are so many options available in bookstores and online for daily devotionals. They are classified by age, gender, and lifestyle. Look for something that you can sit down with for a few minutes. It should have a daily verse along with an explanation on how to apply it to your life. I highly recommend **SheReadsTruth.com** for women and **HeReadsTruth.com** for men as a starting place. You can also try a website such as **Crossway.org** as a place to begin your search. And everything on **AmyLHale.com** will get you started quickly. Take a look today. You won't be disappointed.*

A PRAYER JOURNAL

*If you enjoy writing prompts, a guided prayer journal is a unique and fun option. **Valmariepaper.com** provides a wide array of sizes and styles for men and women to get you praying immediately. Val's journals are small, affordable, and highly effective.*

SUGGESTED READING

S EVERAL books on prayer that I actually *have* enjoyed are:

- *Desperate for Jesus* by John F. Hannah, Salubris Resources (September 1, 2015), ISBN-10: 1680670484
- *The Power of Praying Together* by Stormie Omartian and Jack Hayford, Harvest House Publishers; English Language edition (July 1, 2003) ISBN-10: 0736910034
- *Power of a Praying Woman* by Stormie Omartian (her Power of a Praying series also has editions for men and teens), Harvest House Publishers; Reprint edition (February 1, 2014), ISBN-10: 0736957766
- *Fervent* by Priscilla Shirer, B&H Books (August 1, 2015), ISBN-10: 1433688670
- *Answers to Prayer from George Muller's Narratives* compiled by A.E.C. Brooks CreateSpace Independent Publishing Platform (May 6, 2015), ISBN-10: 1512059269
- *Divine Moments for Men: Everyday Inspiration from God's Word* by Ronald A. Beers and Amy E. Mason, Tyndale House Publishers, Inc. (January 31, 2008), ISBN-10: 1-4143-1227-X
- *Divine Moments for Women: Everyday Inspiration from God's Word* by Ronald A. Beers and Amy E. Mason, Tyndale House Publishers, Inc. (February 1, 2008), ISBN-10: 1414312261

- *Prayers that Avail Much, Vol. 1* by Germaine Copeland, Harrison House (February 1, 2000), ISBN-10: 1577942825

PRAYER FOCUS SHEETS

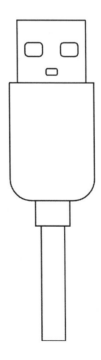

MY PRAYER FOCUS

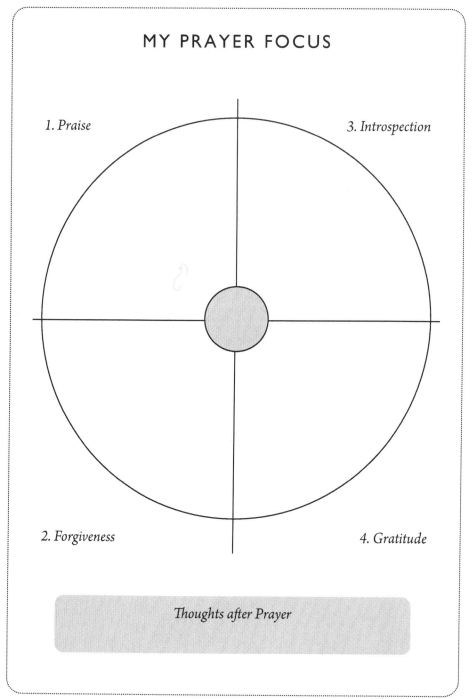

1. Praise

3. Introspection

2. Forgiveness

4. Gratitude

Thoughts after Prayer

Focused Prayer Sheet © Concetta Green, 2017

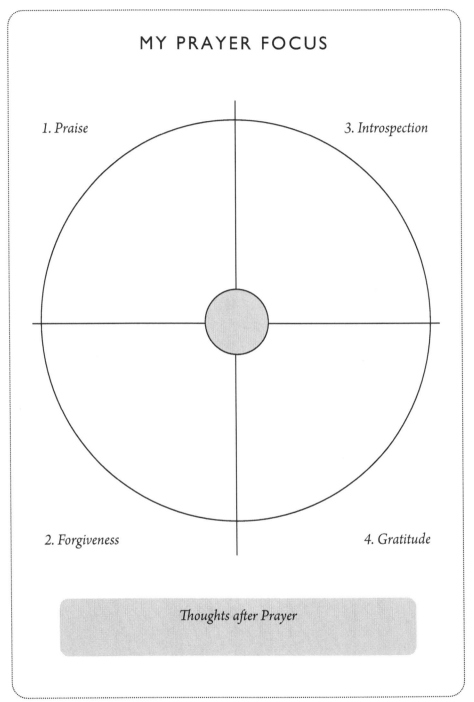

MY PRAYER FOCUS

1. Praise

3. Introspection

2. Forgiveness

4. Gratitude

Thoughts after Prayer

Focused Prayer Sheet © Concetta Green, 2017

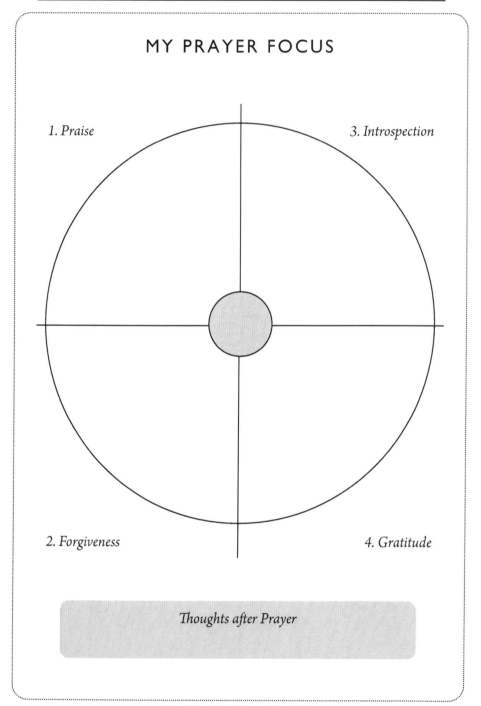

MY PRAYER FOCUS

1. Praise

3. Introspection

2. Forgiveness

4. Gratitude

Thoughts after Prayer

Focused Prayer Sheet © Concetta Green, 2017

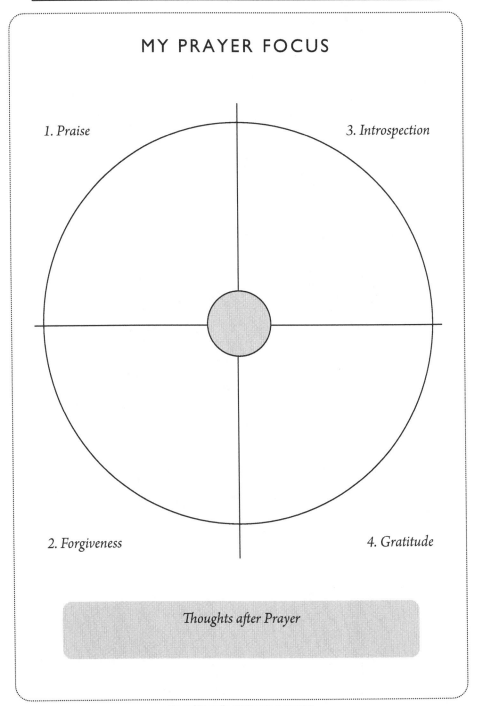

MY PRAYER FOCUS

1. Praise

3. Introspection

2. Forgiveness

4. Gratitude

Thoughts after Prayer

Focused Prayer Sheet © Concetta Green, 2017

ABOUT THE AUTHOR

C ONCETTA Green is a native Bostonian in love with history, documentaries, comedy, and art. After pastoring for seven years alongside her husband, she now enjoys creating tools that make spiritual learning and practice easier and more accessible to all.

STAY CONNECTED

I would love to hear how you have made time for creative prayer. If you enjoyed the book and learned something new, please leave a review sharing your experience on Amazon.com.

You can also share your experience by sending me a message at www.concettagreen.com or connecting with me on Instagram @Concetta_Green using the hashtag:

#TooBusyTooBoredForPrayer